A SPIRIT DAUGHTER WORKBOOK

WRITTEN BY
JILL WINTERSTEEN

FOR THE FULL MOON
THURSDAY, MAY 23, 2024
6:53AM PT

WHY THE FULL MOON

The energies of a Full Moon can bring great change and transformation. This is a time to release what is no longer serving us and stay true to the desires we planted during the New Moon. With the Full Moon being the brightest night of the lunar cycle, there is nowhere to hide in this light. Remember that the light of the Moon actually comes from the Sun as it reflects onto it, flooding out most of its shadows. Similarly, we may come face-to-face with our own shadows. Any internal blockages we may be experiencing are illuminated under this light. The Full Moon is like an accountability partner that says, "Remember those things you wanted to change? Today is the day."

If we look at the bigger picture of the lunar cycle, the work done during a New Moon period before a Full Moon can set us up for a major shift. In contrast with the Full Moon, the New Moon allows us to withdraw from the world and bask in our inner world. During this time, we can discover truths that were perhaps concealed in the subconscious but are now ready to be witnessed. What we

WHY THE FULL MOON

choose to do with this new information for the two weeks until the Full Moon can determine how our manifestations play out for us. This in-between space is for working on our dreams. The New and Waxing Moons bring us an opportunity to integrate new findings about ourselves into our core, overriding outdated programming.

This work of a New Moon is essential in preparing for the Full Moon so that when its radiance comes to illuminate the most hidden depths of the soul, we already know what we want to see shifted out of our lives. Sometimes, this shift happens with ease and everything flows into place. However, when it does not happen smoothly, it is likely due to resistance from within our energetic field formed by self-doubts and old belief systems.

We must remove certain barriers within ourselves to receive what we are trying to manifest with our New Moon intentions. When we block our expansion through limiting beliefs, we also make it more difficult for the people in our lives to support us. Whatever resistance lives in the energetic body can be perceived by others, and even if we vocalize confidence and belief in ourselves, our energy can communicate otherwise. This doubtfulness can even be detected by the Universe, signaling that we still have a bit of work to do until we are ready for a new chapter of our lives. The Full Moon brings us an opportunity to do the work needed to remove these stagnant vibrations.

Every astrological sign has a low side and a high side. These low sides form shadow characteristics that become more noticeable in our own frequencies over a Full Moon. Since the Full Moon always occurs in the sign that is opposite the Sun Season, we can also view the lower frequencies of the Sun sign and understand them at a deeper level. While this self-inquiry may feel challenging and even uncomfortable, it's important to remember these insights are opportunities for growth and are part of your evolution.

Opposing signs form a spectrum of energy between them. On the Full Moon, we can work to release the lower frequencies of each, moving toward the middle. This middle ground is where we can experience the higher sides of the signs and find an equilibrium between the two. There is always a balance to find on a Full Moon. When we can see this as an opportunity instead of a challenge, doors, and pathways to our dreams open. Identifying and transmuting the lower vibrations in this spectrum of energy helps us release barriers and blocks that prevent us from manifesting our highest visions. When we find balance among these energies, we can fully realize our dreams.

Full Moons have a reputation for being times of intense energy when everything feels amplified. While this may make us feel exposed and raw, we should remember there is a silver lining to this intensity. When our challenges and uncomfortable feelings are amplified, so is our potential. Nothing exists in a vacuum. However, while this empowering force may be effective for doing inner work and work within a spiritual realm, we should give ourselves a bit of grace during this period and allow for times of rest and restoration. Remember to be compassionate and patient with yourself. If you can fully align with the opportunity each Full Moon brings to create change in your life, you can break through limiting barriers and shift your life in any direction you choose.

SAGITTARIUS FULL MOON

Sagittarius is the eternal student of the zodiac, forever wandering the globe in search of new knowledge and perspectives. This energy compels us to be curious and leave our comfort zones. It encourages us to open our minds to new perspectives and experiences. It also asks us to take the road less traveled. The energy of Sagittarius is not concerned with the familiar. It craves newness from every angle. Boredom is the death of Sagittarius. Routines and predictability have no place in this energy. Sagittarius wants us to feel confused. It asks us to throw everything we know up in the air and allow the pieces to land where they may. It's only by shuffling life into disarray that we can connect the dots in new ways, finding connections we may have missed if we had kept everything neat and tidy.

Sagittarius also represents hope. It compels us to take leaps of faith, trusting that the best will unfold. This energy helps us focus on the good and, in that attention, cultivate more positive vibrations throughout life. This energy dares us to take a chance, even if we don't know the outcome. Sagittarius teaches us that we can always find the higher meaning in any situation, even those that don't go according to plan. We never need to fear what may happen because we can always find the silver lining if we try hard enough. We do not need to take the familiar road out of fear of the unknown. Sagittarius wants us to walk into unfamiliar territory with the inner confidence that the best-case scenario will occur, even if we have to find it.

This Full Moon is a time to acknowledge where you're making fear-based decisions. It's a time to become aware of routines and ruts that you've formed to cling to the familiar. It's also a time to face your fears of the unknown and take leaps of faith that help you grow. Over this Full Moon, remind yourself that the Universe is always looking out for you and ask yourself how you can shake things up a bit. Step out of your comfort zone and align with the energy of hope to heal

SAGITTARIUS FULL MOON

the part of yourself scared of the unknown. Acknowledge your fears when they come and learn from them, but resist their control. Fear is an interesting emotion. It serves us well during crucial times of our lives but also blocks our growth when it governs all of our decisions. When feeling fear, ask yourself if it is really warranted. Is there a genuine threat to your well-being, or is fear misplaced? What fear is essential to keep you safe, and what fear is blocking your growth or preventing you from following your intuition?

The Sagittarius Full Moon has the power to help you understand which fears need to stay and which ones should go. It also opens up the door to believing the best can happen. We spend much of our time "what if-ing" ourselves and envisioning the worst-case scenario. This catastrophic thinking only serves to block our ability to manifest and recognize best-case scenarios. Worrying about the future does not help you in any way. It may feel like you are preparing for different scenarios or controlling outcomes, but really you are just depleting your energy. The best way to prepare for any potentially negative situations is to stay fully present. When you remain present, you have your full energy and attention to respond to anything life hands you. Being present and assuming the best will happen is key to working with this Full Moon. Challenge yourself to remain in this state of mind for at least the day. When intrusive thoughts enter, counter them with affirmations that state the opposite. Challenge your worries and fears with the help of this Moon and ask yourself if you can heal these fears by focusing on the positive in your life.

Creating a positive mindset does not mean you ignore negative feelings or events. Sagittarius teaches us that there is nothing negative or positive on our journeys. There are only lessons. We can find the higher meaning in everything if we are willing to look. Address your negative emotions, but also take the time to heal them. Heal them with optimism and the willingness to find the silver lining in even your most challenging times. Heal them with hope for a brighter future and the inner knowing that we are all evolving together. Sagittarius teaches us that life is always handing us wisdom in different forms. We are continually growing and evolving. Some of these lessons may not be what we consciously want, and they may even leave us with negativity, but ultimately they help us become the person we are meant to be in this life. Let this Full Moon help you find a deeper meaning to every event in your life, and then let this knowledge heal you.

Throughout this Full Moon, notice what it feels like to operate from a vibration of fear. Notice how fear affects your decisions and your ability to listen to your intuition. Your inner knowledge is grounded in the present. It comes through quickly and feels like a flash of brilliance or insight. Fear, on the other hand, comes with much overthinking. It can be visceral but leads you on a downward spiral, where you can no longer hear yourself. All you can hear is fear. On this Full Moon, learn about your fears and understand how they control your narratives. What stories do your fears tell you? How do your fears impact your ability to listen to and be guided by your inner knowledge? Notice how fear has controlled you in the past, and commit to not allowing it to control you in the future. Step into unknown territory by making decisions based on your assumption the best will happen instead of those based in fear. Believe in yourself and believe in all the good in your life, then know this belief will call in the energy you need to evolve in the best way possible.

SAGITTARIUS MOON X
GEMINI SUN

Of all the opposing signs, Sagittarius and Gemini are the most similar. They both ask us to be curious, widen our perspectives, and connect with others to learn, unlearn, and grow. We are working with both of these energies today, as the Sun sits in Gemini and the Moon sits in Sagittarius. As these two oppose each other for our Full Moon, we are given the opportunity to shed both Gemini's and Sagittarius's lower vibrations and embrace the higher ones. With the power of the Full Moon, we shift stagnant energy that has blocked our efforts to grow and manifest our intentions. Full Moons are powerful times for release. It's up to you to decide what you want to shift this day and allow the Moon to help you make these changes.

While you may not be a Gemini or Sagittarius Sun or Moon sign, all of us hold these energies within our energetic fields, and we all have the opportunity to work with these vibrations on the Full Moon. Gemini governs our communication. This energy shows up when we are exchanging information and connecting with the world around us. When we align with the higher vibrations of Gemini, we remain open-minded and curious. We understand that our knowledge is limited and everyone is our teacher. Gemini's highest vibrations are that of a researcher: inquisitive, nonjudgmental, and open to all possibilities.

Gemini's energy moves quickly and allows us to immediately scan an environment, a project, or even an email for details. When we align with the opportunities Gemini presents, we become fascinated by the world around us, desiring to know everything we can about its mysteries. We become the observer, which in turn makes us less reactive to our emotions. Gemini's high side allows us to detach from our emotions while remaining present with them. When we are less reactive to our feelings, they lose the power to control us, becoming merely information. This nonreactive state allows us to continue learning without closing our minds due to fear, misunderstanding, or anxiety. It also allows us to receive messages from the Universe. When we are open to different forms of communication, we open ourselves to receiving signs from the world around us. Gemini's energy can help us receive much-needed information on our paths if we are willing to acknowledge it.

Every energy has a low and a high side. Gemini's low, or shadow, side includes judgment, close-mindedness, and ungrounded energy. When we align with this side, our nervous energy takes over and we become fearful of the world around us. The mind races from one thought to another, with nothing to center it. We react to our emotions either with anxiety or by numbing ourselves so we feel nothing at all. In this state, we cannot correctly process our feelings, and they wreak havoc behind the scenes. Suppressed emotions can cause disturbances in sleep, eating, or even the ability to digest food and ideas. In an attempt to balance this lower vibratory state of Gemini, we often overanalyze and overthink everything. To control the anxiety, we inundate ourselves and the people around us with questions while we look for answers. We ignore intuition and insist that logic is the only way. We also miss signs and messages that can give us information from the Universe. We disconnect from universal wisdom and our inner knowledge.

SAGITTARIUS MOON
X GEMINI SUN

If you find yourself aligning with the lower frequencies of Gemini on this Full Moon, or at any time, ground yourself through your breath and body. Do some yoga to connect with your physical energy, getting yourself out of your head. Try to feel your emotions, even if they scare you. Rely on the communication Gemini offers to journal, talk to a friend, or even just listen as someone talks to you. Challenge yourself to open your mind and suspend judgment, even if for a moment. Feel your intuition guiding you and trust that all the answers you need in this moment will easily come to you. You do not need to worry about the future or try to control it. You just need to be open to communicating with yourself and the world around you in the present moment.

Sagittarius, much like Gemini, encourages us to explore. This energy inspires us to travel, embrace new cultures, and open our minds to new realities. The high side of Sagittarius is optimistic and full of joy. It sees the world as one integrated whole where everything is connected. When we align with this higher vibration, we trust that everything will work out how it's meant to, even in the face of adversity. Sagittarius's high-side energy allows us to see life as a perpetual journey of unraveling truths. There is no endpoint, and we can never exhaust the world's knowledge. There are always new truths to learn and new perspectives to incorporate into our own understanding.

The high side of Sagittarius shows us the infinite potential of our consciousness and encourages us to expand it with every opportunity. In this frequency, we become open to receiving new truths and taking leaps of faith. We trust the journey of life and know that even if we stumble, we are still learning. Life becomes an evolving experience where there are no failures, no wrong turns, and no mistakes. There are just new realities to encounter that will expand our consciousness to new levels. With each level, we evolve our energy and broaden our connection with the Universe.

As joyful and wonderful as the energy of Sagittarius is, it too has a low side. Sagittarius, in its shadow side, loses faith. When we align with this vibration, we lose trust in ourselves, our paths, and even the Universe. We question the meaning of our existence and allow ourselves to fall into a downward spiral of questions that even the greatest philosophers cannot answer. Sagittarius, in its lowest state, causes us to experience an existential crisis, preventing us from moving forward in life. We become stuck in an infinite loop of contemplation. We fail to launch into something new and question the point of everything. We question the meaning of our lives and the meaning of everything that has happened to us. We expect disappointment and take a pessimistic view of our journeys. Fear-based decisions control us, and we may even start assuming worst-case scenarios, focusing on the negative. Life begins to feel pointless in this vibration.

If you find yourself in this frequency of Sagittarius, take even the smallest step forward into something new. Even if you cannot take a huge leap, find some way to bring new energy into your life. Make a breakthrough in your energy by taking a chance in any direction. Remind yourself of the higher meaning of your

SAGITTARIUS MOON
X GEMINI SUN

life and focus on the positive of a past event, even if it's challenging to find it. Take a broad look at your life in the context of the planet and see the whole point of it all.

Another low side of Sagittarius is self-righteousness and judgment. When we align with this side, we assume our experiences have made us more knowledgeable than those around us. We seek to bestow our thoughts and opinions on others, even if those thoughts and opinions are unsolicited. We believe that everyone wants to hear our views because our views are the best. This type of energy shuts down our ability to receive new information. It closes our minds and makes us judge anyone who does not agree with us. It can also cause us to judge those who are different, seeing them not as teachers but rather as threats to our understanding of the world. If you find yourself aligning with this side, try on a different viewpoint. See something through a new lens or perhaps through another person's eyes. If you find yourself feeling judgmental, try to see the world from another perspective. You can also try a judgment detox. Write down all of your judgments, including those of yourself, and notice any patterns. What are your habitual ways of judging? Where do they come from? Next, identify how the way you judge yourself impacts the way you judge others. By bringing awareness to your judgments, you shift them and encourage a new way of perceiving the world.

Know that it's ok to align with the lower frequencies of these signs. We all have experienced these vibrations to some degree. Notice if you are judging yourself, and instead practice compassion for your journey. Take the opportunity this Full Moon offers to notice any of these patterns in yourself, then shift them. It may feel uncomfortable to step into a new vibration. But know that, over time, the new frequencies you cultivate will feel like home.

ASPECTS

Sun in Gemini

Moon in Sagittarius

Mercury in Taurus

Venus in Taurus

Mars in Aries

Jupiter in Taurus

Saturn in Pisces

Uranus in Taurus

Neptune in Pisces

Pluto in Aquarius

North Node in Aries

Chiron in Aries

ASPECTS

The Flower Moon in Sagittarius has many aspects. There are a few other cosmic energies at play this day that influence this Moon. The Moon forms an exact sextile aspect with Pluto in Aquarius, while the Sun in Gemini forms an exact trine with the small planet. Pluto's energy helps us heal from our past. It places our trauma against the larger background of our overall life cycle. It also helps us understand the ongoing cycles of our lives, including the many births and deaths our energy has endured.

Pluto's influence on this Full Moon is powerful. Pluto in Aquarius helps us heal parts of ourselves that prevent us from embracing our potential and unique genius. The Sagittarius Full Moon is an invitation to look at old wounds that prevent you from expanding or taking a leap of faith. Is there something from your past that is holding you back? And what do you need to help you process it?

Often, we hold on to the past because our mind or energy still hasn't integrated the experience. We may still be trying to figure something out or wrap our heads around an event. We may also need to dive deep into the emotional processing needed to let go of something. Perhaps there was an associated emotion that we could not confront or didn't have the tools to unravel. When we remain attached to the past, it steals our energy. It takes away from our resources that we could use to move forward and grow.

Over this Full Moon, with the help of Pluto, look at what is holding you back from truly stepping into your power. What is preventing you from speaking your truth or taking up the space you deserve? What is holding you back from creating your visions and building the life you know is yours? Then listen to the answers, and if it's your attachments to your past that are holding you back, align with this Moon to do the work needed to release them. Understand your past from a higher vantage point, one that can help you find the deeper meaning of your experience. See it as part of your overall energetic evolution, even if it was challenging.

Once you free yourself from your past by finding the lesson, higher meaning, and even redirection, then you'll be free to walk into an expanded future. Take a leap of faith this Sagittarius Full Moon and detach from your past pain. It may feel scary to be without something that may have been with you for years. Our pain can serve as a familiar landscape. Ask yourself who you would be without it.

Jupiter, the planet of expansion and ruler of Sagittarius, sits right next to Venus in the final degree of Taurus, this Full Moon. The two will enter Gemini together in a matter of days. This conjunction expands our hearts. It's a reminder to always love yourself and that love will ultimately help you find your power. This is also a grounding energy that has the potential to help you find your breath and body as you move through this fast-paced Moon.

Spend time this Full Moon connecting with things you love. Walk in the sunrise, smell the flowers around you, or have lunch with a friend. Slow down and enjoy life through little moments of bliss today. Let this heart connection expand you and help you release what no longer serves you. Say goodbye to anything that doesn't resonate with your heart and let it lead you forward. Your heart always knows the path you need to walk. Listen to it today and allow this intuition to ground you.

FULL MOON HOROSCOPES

LOVE CONQUERS ALL

ARIES

This Full Moon lands in your 9th house of travel and philosophy and it's a promising moment for you to explore the big, wide, world. Whether you're hopping on a plane or finishing a graduate degree...it's time to celebrate the things you've been learning that are giving you hope. You can also think back to similar themes that might've been just beginning in December 2023, and notice how things are now coming full circle within your desire to learn and go on big adventures. The world is your oyster around this Full Moon!

TAURUS

This Full Moon lands in your 8th house of shared resources and it's a time to show gratitude for your symbiotic relationships. There could be an influx of money that finds its way to you, or otherwise you're just feeling especially cared for on an emotional level. It's important to practice your worthiness around this date and trust that you're receiving what you're owed. You can also think back to similar themes that might've been just beginning in December 2023, and notice how things are now coming full circle within your connections with others.

GEMINI

This Full Moon lands in your 7th house of committed partnerships and it's the most beautiful Full Moon of the year to celebrate the people you love! If you're single, you might not be for long. There is an abundance of optimism and sweetness surrounding your one on one relationships now, so lean into the people that feel like an adventure. You can also think back to similar themes that might've been just beginning in December 2023, and notice how things are now coming full circle within your partnerships. Dance to the beat of your own drums together under the stars!

CANCER

This Full Moon lands in your 6th house of work and routines and it's an especially hopeful moment for your wellness. If you've been trying to get your health in order, you should be feeling especially hopeful about the progress you've made thus far. Your coworkers might be bringing gifts your way as well, so the 9-5 is less likely to feel like a grind at this time, and more like a place of gratitude. You can also think back to similar themes that might've been just beginning in December 2023, and notice how things are now coming full circle within your work dynamics and daily tasks.

LEO

This Full Moon lands in your 5th house of creativity and romance and it's quite the positive omen for your passion projects. You're likely to be feeling the love around this date, so if someone asks you out– say YES! It's also a wonderful time to celebrate yourself, and the inner-child work you've been doing, so buy yourself flowers or the popsicles you loved as a kid. You can also think back to similar themes that might've been just beginning in December 2023, and notice how things are now coming full circle within your passion projects and creativity. Embrace play today and let your younger self enjoy it all!

VIRGO

This Full Moon lands in your 4th house of home and family and is helping you to embrace the tender, loving care of your root systems. Whether you're tackling a renovation project or welcoming a new member into your family (or both!), let

LOVE CONQUERS ALL

this Full Moon be a moment of hopefulness for your core unit. You can also think back to similar themes that might've been just beginning in December 2023, and notice how things are now coming full circle within your home and family life.

LIBRA

This Full Moon lands in your 3rd house of local community and will likely have you buzzing around town like a busy bee! You're feeling optimistic around this date, exploring your community and perhaps learning new things about your friends and/or siblings. You can also think back to similar themes that might've been just beginning for you in December 2023, and notice how things are now coming full circle within your immediate conversations. Lean into exuberant exchanges.

SCORPIO

This Full Moon lands in your 2nd house of values and has you expanding your ideas of support. You could receive a raise around this date, or decide to move forward on a new money making venture. You can also think back to similar themes that might've been just beginning in December 2023, and notice how things are now coming full circle within your financial resources. This is a very lucky Full Moon for your wallet, and have no doubt that it reflects your hard work.

SAGITTARIUS

This Full Moon lands in your 1st house of self and is the best Full Moon of the year for you. People will be admiring you far and wide and your charm is likely to be off the charts. If you appreciate comedy, this is the perfect time to go to a show or perform your own! You can also think back to similar themes that might've been just beginning in December 2023, and notice how things are now coming full circle within your first impressions and personality as a whole.

CAPRICORN

This Full Moon lands in your 12th house and will bring expanse to your behind the scenes projects. Whether you're deciding to deep dive on a spiritual journey or celebrating love shared in privacy, this optimistic Full Moon is best experienced away from the public eye. You can also think back to similar themes that might've been just beginning in December 2023, and notice how things are now coming full circle within your still gestating plans. Let yourself feel excited for what is soon to be born!

AQUARIUS

This Full Moon lands in your 11th house of community and will bring great expanse to the groups that claim you as a proud member. You could be joining a new club, attending a conference, or otherwise aligning yourself with people that share your same values around this Full Moon. You can also think back to similar themes that might've been just beginning in December 2023, and notice how things are now coming full circle within your hopes and dreams in the collective.

PISCES

This Full Moon lands in your 10th house of career and people will be wanting to see and be seen with you! This Full Moon is extremely abundant and optimistic, and that energy will shine loudly for you at the office. Let your work transport people. You can also think back to similar themes that might've been just beginning in December 2023, and notice how things are now coming full circle within the legacy you hope to leave behind.

SAGITTARIUS LUNAR FLOW

Sagittarius rules the hips and thighs. She also rules the hip flexors, including the psoas, a muscle that runs from the mid-spine to the front of the hips. It is primarily responsible for helping us walk. Energetically, the psoas controls the flight-or-fight response. It allows us to either curl up in a ball or charge forward. It contracts when we are feeling fear. Often, fear stagnates here, affecting our ability to change.

During a Sagittarius Full Moon, we want to open the hips and psoas so we are free to walk into new territory, both mentally and physically. Through opening this area, we release fear and permit ourselves to step into our destiny.

SUN SALUTATION WITH LUNGE: 3 ROUNDS

Stand at the top of your mat. Inhale, stretch your arms overhead > Exhale, fold forward > Inhale, lengthen out your back > Exhale, step your right foot back, lower your knee to the ground > Inhale, lift your arms and torso up into a low lunge > Exhale, step back to Plank Pose, and lower > Inhale, reach your chest up for Cobra Pose, legs on the ground > Exhale, Downward Dog Pose. Stay here for 5 breaths and feel your entire body expand. On the exhale, step your right foot forward, lower your back knee to the ground > Inhale, reach your arms and torso to the sky > Exhale, lower your arms, and step to the top of the mat > Inhale, lengthen through your spine > Exhale, fold forward > Inhale, come all the way up to standing, reaching arms overhead > Exhale, hands to your heart. Pause for a moment and feel yourself centered throughout your body. On your third round, remain in Downward Dog and breathe for 5 breaths.

CRESCENT LUNGE WITH TWIST

From Downward Dog, step your left foot forward into a Lunge Pose. Your back heel will lift from the ground and your leg will stay straight. Bend deeply into your front knee as you tilt your tailbone toward the ground. Reach your arms toward the sky and send your breath into your hips. After 5 breaths, reach your right arm forward and left arm back, twisting to the left. Breathe here for 5 breaths, then place your right hand down, 12 inches from your left foot, and reach your left arm up for a deeper twist. Release both hands to the ground and step back into a vinyasa or Downward Dog. Repeat on the right side.

WARRIOR 2 > REVERSE WARRIOR > EXTENDED WARRIOR (BOTH SIDES)

From Downward Dog, step your left foot forward for Warrior 2. Spin your back foot flat on the ground at a 45-degree angle inward and rotate your torso to the right side of the mat, reaching your arms to either side. Bend your front knee, pressing it out to the left.

Take 5 breaths here, opening up your pelvis and grounding down through your legs. After 5 breaths, rotate your left palm to the sky and arch your back for Reverse Warrior. Reach your left arm in line with your ear and stretch open the left side of your body. Spend 5 breaths here, then lift your torso. Place your left elbow on your left knee for Extended Warrior. Reach your right arm overhead in line with your ear. Spend 5 breaths here, then place your hands back to the ground, stepping back into a vinyasa or Downward Dog for 5 breaths before switching sides.

TRIANGLE > HALF MOON > CHAPASANA

From Downward Dog, step your left foot forward. Angle your back foot at 45 degrees and line up your arch with your front heel. Lift your torso up and straighten your front leg. Reach your arms out to either side and hinge forward into Triangle Pose. Place your left hand on the ground on the outside of your left foot or on your shin, then rotate your torso to the right. Stretch and reach upward through your right arm, feeling one long line of energy from fingertip to fingertip. Stay here for 5 breaths, then place your left hand about 12 inches in front of your left foot, bending your front knee. Launch forward into Half Moon Pose, lifting your back leg and pressing through that heel. Your toes will be facing to the right. Find your balance here, then slowly begin to bend your right leg and catch hold of the top of your foot for chapasana. Try to keep your leg parallel to the ground as you open the front of your hip by kicking your foot into your hand. Remain here for 5 breaths, then slowly release to Downward Dog, switching sides.

LIZARD POSE > HALF SPLITS POSE

From Downward Dog, step your left foot outside your left hand. Lower your back knee and sink your hips forward. Feel the front of your right thigh opening as you breathe. If you'd like to go deeper, you can lower to your elbows. After 5 breaths, bring your front foot back in line with your front hip. Straighten that leg out for Half Splits Pose. Have your hips directly over your back knee and fold forward over your straight leg. Use blocks under your hands if you need to. Keep your back as straight as possible as you fold. After 5 breaths, return to Downward Dog and switch sides.

PIGEON POSE

Return to Downward Dog through a vinyasa or by stepping back. Then take your left knee to your left wrist for Pigeon Pose. Go easy on your knee. If you feel any pain, do Thread the Needle Pose, a Pigeon modification. Carefully lay down your left leg and stretch your right leg back. Before folding, press up through your hands and arch your back a bit, stretching through the front of your body. On exhale, fold forward over your leg and remain here for 10 breaths. On each inhale, send your breath into your hips, encouraging them to open. On exhale, release a bit more. After 10 breaths, slowly switch sides.

SAVASANA

Release onto the floor, lying with your palms up and eyes closed. Feel your body alive with fresh energy circulating freely through it.

SAGITTARIUS MEDITATION

The Sagittarius Full Moon is a powerful time to face and transform fears. Fear has a way of living in our bodies. While it is often at the forefront of our minds, it also can subconsciously change our perceptions and behavior. We can hold fear in different areas of the physical, energetic, and emotional body. Fear, though, always has something to teach us. It can bring us wisdom and help us understand ourselves on a deeper level. It can shed light on blocks and obstacles that prevent us from manifesting our dreams.

When we embrace fear with an open mind, we can understand it. In that understanding, we can take away any power it has over us. Fear may always come to pay us a visit, but we do not have to let it change our course of action or deter our plans in any way. We simply need to listen to it, acknowledge it, and move it out of our bodies. Through facing our fears, we begin to control them and life's course.

The following guided meditation is meant to help you understand your fears and shift them out of your body, making room for your inspiration and courage to blossom.

SAGITTARIUS MEDITATION

TALKING WITH YOUR FEARS

The first step in transforming fears is to understand them. Your fear has something to say and wants to be heard. The best thing you can do is listen to it with an open mind. Once your fears are heard, they become less demanding. They are more easily moved away from you as they quiet down, knowing they have expressed their concerns.

Begin in a seated position with your spine upright, eyes closed, and hands placed lightly in your lap. Observe your breath, watching the inhale and exhale. Place all of your focus on feeling your breath in this moment as it enters and leaves your body. Know that you can always place your focus here to calm yourself down and center your energy.

Feel if any fear is living in your body. Observe any tightness or feelings of restlessness in your physical form. Breathe into them and allow them open. Then ask yourself, What fears am I feeling today? Allow your fears to rise up by staying centered on your breath and grounded in your body. As your fears emerge, stay open to them. Become increasingly aware if you are tightening areas of your body and send your breath to them. Attempt to remain open in your physical form even as fears swirl around in your mind.

Choose one fear to focus on. Ask this fear, What do you want to teach me? What are your concerns? What do you think you see that I am blind to? What is your worst-case scenario? Be open to these answers both in your body and in your mind. Stay centered on your breath for a few moments as your fear talks to you. As it speaks, be curious about what your fear wants to teach you.

After you've heard your fear, ask another set of questions. Ask your fear, What will it take for you to trust the process of our life? What will it take for you to feel supported and at ease in our journey? How can I help you surrender to what you can't control? Once again, focus on your breath and give space for your fears to answer.

Slowly open your eyes, then take your pen and write down the answers to the second set of questions, letting them develop even more as you write them onto the paper. Focus on trust and surrender here, and ask your fear once again how it can move toward these vibrations. After you finish writing, return to your seated position with your eyes closed, and focus on your inhale and exhale. Stay here for a few moments, grounding your energy. Then let your nervous system settle as you process your answers.

Feel more at ease in your body and in control of your life. If your fears continue to pop up , sit down and have a conversation with them. Allow them to be heard, then move them toward trust in your life and your path.

CIRCLE SET UP

On this Full Moon, we are working with the elements of Fire from Sagittarius and Air from Gemini. Air stokes the flames of Fire, allowing these two elements to feed off of each other and combine their energy. Air inspires us, helping us shift and change. Fire helps us burn away anything we no longer want in our lives. This Full Moon is about movement and change. Feel into this energy when creating your space. Make sure there is good airflow and plenty of room for movement if needed. Also, choose a space that feels grounded and connected to Mother Earth. Fire needs an anchor to keep from blowing out of control. You can practice your rituals outside, close to the ground. Or you can choose a space that contains the Wood element. If these are not available to you, place plants and crystals in your circle to bring the Earth inside. You can practice alone or in a community; it's entirely up to you. Sagittarius is a very social sign, so you may be called to practice with others. If this is the case, gather with people who make you feel safe and encourage you to expand into your potential.

Incorporate the rest of the elements into your circle, along with Earth. If possible, build a fire outside, which you can use later for releasing energy. You can also light candles in your space. For Air, incorporate auric sprays, feathers to fan smudge sticks, and even wind chimes to hear the air moving around you. Place crystals in the middle of the circle and around the perimeter. Crystals that align with the energy of Sagittarius are Turquoise, Red Jasper, and Aventurine. These crystals will bring you serendipity and give you the confidence to make a big leap forward. Crystals for Gemini are Agate, Apophyllite, and Chrysocolla. These crystals will help you communicate with your higher Self and become your own teacher. You can also incorporate flowers of both Sagittarius and Gemini into your space, including narcissus, carnations, ranunculus, and daffodils to represent the Earth element. Bring in the element of Water through a room diffuser, a vase, or a metal bowl containing water. Gather all of your supplies and build your circle.

TURQUOISE   RED JASPER   AVENTURINE

AGATE   APOPHYLLITE   CHRYSOCOLLA

Create an outline with your objects, anchoring the four directions—north, south, east, and west—with either a crystal or candle. If you are creating an altar, set it up in the westerly part of the circle, as this direction helps energies release. An altar can contain objects that help infuse wisdom into your space. It can hold crystals, flowers, letters of intentions, and pictures of loved ones or spirit guides. Altars can anchor the energy of a space and give a focal point as you practice. Crystal grids can also anchor the energy and project it outward through its formation. If setting up a crystal grid, have it in the center of the circle, choosing a generator or tower crystal for the center.

CIRCLE SET UP

Once you've set the perimeter, cleanse the area with a dried herb. Juniper is a wonderful cleansing herb that also provides protection. Begin cleansing at the easterly point, moving to the south, west, north, then back to the east. Imagine a white light encasing the circle, protecting it from any external energies. Before any guests enter, cleanse each one of them and then yourself, wafting the smoke around the entire body, including the soles of the feet. Once you have all entered the circle, pause for a moment to let the energy settle before you begin.

Follow your intuitive guidance when leading a circle. Begin with each member introducing themself. Talk about the astrological energy of the day and how it is affecting each one of you. Share and learn from each other about your unique experiences with the Full Moon's energy. Give plenty of space for each person to speak. Follow your conversation with the meditation practice in this book to calm the mind. You can then explore the rest of the practices. Do them alone, but share as much or as little as you want with the rest of the group. Go over the questions and continue to learn from each other's perspectives.

After you've completed the practices, take three pieces of paper. On one, write something you are releasing this Full Moon. On the second, write an intention you are calling in through the element of Air. On the third, write what you are grateful for tonight. Gather all the releasing notes and either burn them (safely) or rip them to shreds. Gather the intention notes and place them under a crystal in the most easterly corner of your home. Leave them there for a week. For the gratitude notes, pass yours to the person on the left, who passes theirs to the person on their left, and so on; everyone will take their neighbor's home. Sharing in others' gratitude is a beautiful way to merge our energy with the collective's. If you are practicing alone, place your gratitude note somewhere you can see it every day. End the circle by giving thanks to everyone who attended, including yourself, and to yourself for showing up.

CARD READING

20

CARD PULLED: **CARD PULLED:**   **CARD PULLED:**

Reading Cards is a beautiful way to access your intuition and tap into your, and the Universe's, higher wisdom. Anyone can pull cards, as long as you are willing to receive the information they provide. You need no prior experience, or training, just an open and clear mind.

You may use any cards you like for this practice, including but not limited to: Tarot Cards, Animal Medicine Cards, Oracle Cards or any Affirmation Cards. You also can pull cards from a few decks to gain different perspectives. If you are new to card pulling, try to ask only one deck the same question, as asking different decks the same question can become quite confusing. Below are some general guidelines on how to pull cards. Please improvise as needed and above anything else, listen to your intuition.

CLEAR YOUR MIND

A settled, grounded mind is essential for pulling cards. The last thing you want is random thoughts running around when you are trying to receive clear answers from yourself. Practice the breath work and meditation in this workbook to prepare and settle your mind. You may also clear your mind using sound frequencies through singing bowls. These can either be crystal or metal bowls. Play the bowl, or bowls, for about 3-5 minutes to help rid your mind of external noise as you focus on the harmony of the sound.

CARD READING

PICK YOUR DECK

There are many different decks out there. You can choose as many as you like. Know, though, that they each provide you a different energy or medicine. Tarot Cards are the most popular and should be used carefully. Although very useful, Tarot cards can give the wrong impression if you interpret them harshly. Animal Medicine cards offer different types of messages from the animal realm which can help align with the spirit of nature. These cards give you the medicine you need to apply to your situation or question. Affirmation cards provide you with guidance in the form of words or phrases. When reading these cards, it is best to meditate on what the affirmation means for you. It is also helpful to repeat the affirmation a few times and see how it makes you feel. There are many other cards you can experiment with, like Goddess Cards, Angel Cards, and so on. The important thing to remember with any card is that they each have different angles and sides. There are often a few interpretations of the same card.

SHUFFLE

Shuffle the cards the easiest way for you. Some cards are smaller and can be shuffled like a regular deck of playing cards, while others with take some effort. If all else fails, spread them out on the floor in front of you then regather them. Keep a clear mind while shuffling. You can also repeat " I am open to receiving guidance and intuition." Refrain from asking your questions until the next step.

SAGITTARIS CARD QUESTIONS

You are free to ask the deck any questions you need answers to on this Full Moon. The following questions are meant to help you harness the energy of Sagittarius through the cards to clarify some of these energies in your mind. This is a three-part card reading, where you'll ask the deck three questions. Before beginning, spread your freshly shuffled cards in a wide arc in front of you. Use your left middle finger to choose the card, first waving your hand slowly over the cards. You'll feel a magnetic pull, or slight tingle, in your fingertip when you hover over the right card. Chose one card at a time, taking a moment to breathe in between questions. Keep the cards flipped over until you pull all three.

What energy will help me release fear, pain, or the past?

What energy will help me expand from my heart's space?

What energy will help me see and embody the bigger vision of my life?

TAKE THEM IN

Once you have your cards, flip them over. Before looking up their meaning, sit with them for a moment and allow them to speak to you. Intuit your own meaning and interpretation of the card. What is the card trying to tell you? What are you trying to tell yourself? After a few moments with the cards, look up their meaning. Sit with that information, merging it with your intuitive meaning of the cards.

As with everything, enjoy this process. Do not worry if you are doing it right or wrong. Just follow your intuition, and trust the journey. Accept the cards you are dealt and use their energy wisely to help guide you when you need it the most.

just like the Moon,

you have to trust that each
phase of your life will be more
beautiful than the last.

- spirit daughter

SAGITTARIUS PRACTICES

The Full Flower Moon in Sagittarius allows us to confront our fears and change our response to them. The energy of Sagittarius helps us think positively and take leaps into the unknown with an open mind. This Full Moon is an opportunity to break free of fears holding you back from manifesting the life you want. It's also a time to identify what common fears come up within you and where they come from. The world has been a chaotic place for the past two years. It's natural to have fear around situations that once seemed safe. It's also natural for your mind to spiral downward into a sea of negativity fueled by headlines, social media posts, and other sources of information that focus on the negativity in the world.

This Full Moon is a time to take your power back and control your fear. It's a time to decide what you will focus on and raise your vibration in the process. Sagittarius teaches us to assume the best will happen. But before we get into that mindset, we need to address the part that assumes the worst will happen. We need to sit our fears down, have a conversation with them, learn from them, and release them.

What are your common triggers for fearful thoughts and feelings?

_____

_____

_____

_____

_____

_____

_____

_____

_____

Where does fear live in your body? What areas tense up or react when you are in a state of fear?

_____

_____

_____

_____

_____

_____

_____

SAGITTARIUS PRACTICES

Experiencing fear is a natural part of being human. In some cases, fear serves us very well and keeps us safe from harm. When fear has no real purpose, though, it can block our growth and enjoyment of life. Fear can prevent us from experiencing all that life has to offer. It can keep us trapped in a web of perceived threats when, in reality, we are safe. It can also cause us to focus on negativity in the world and manifest negative situations in our own lives.

The first step in confronting your fears is asking if they are valid. Are you in an unsafe situation? And if so, how can you use your fear as fuel to get yourself to safety? Real fear lives in the body. It is instinctive. If you are fearing the future or imagining worst-case scenarios, then you may not be in immediate danger. If this is the case, it's time to face your fears and release them, freeing yourself to think positively.

What positive energies can you notice around you when you feel fear? What can you focus on to raise your vibration and free yourself of fear?

_____

_____

_____

_____

_____

_____

_____

_____

_____

_____

_____

What practices bring you into the present moment where fear does not live? What can take you out of future visions that portray negative outcomes and instead remind you that everything is ok right now?

_____

_____

_____

_____

SAGITTARIUS PRACTICES

_____

_____

_____

_____

_____

_____

When dealing with your fears, it's also helpful to look at the evidence. When in a fearful state, we can forget to look around to see if our fears are valid. We may assume the worst without any proof that the worst is happening or will happen. When you are facing fears about yourself, your abilities, your future, or even your interactions with others, ask yourself if there is evidence of their validity.

What evidence is available to prove your fears are true? What is available to prove they are false?

_____

_____

_____

_____

_____

_____

_____

_____

_____

_____

_____

_____

_____

_____

SAGITTARIUS PRACTICES

In confronting your fears, it's important to ask where the fear comes from. Fear can be left over from past events that no longer remain in the present. Fear often does not understand time. If you experienced a trauma in your past, your present mind can think the trauma is still occurring. You need to tell yourself the threat has passed and you are now in a new reality. This process can take time and even require the guidance of a trusted therapist, but you can see how the past is just that: the past. You no longer need to live in fear of something that has already happened. Let yourself know that it is over and you no longer need to fear it.

Do you fear events that have already occurred? What can help you understand they are over and will not happen again?

_____

_____

_____

_____

_____

_____

_____

_____

_____

What will help you heal these fears and focus on the present, where there is no evidence of your fears existing?

_____

_____

_____

_____

_____

_____

_____

_____

_____

SAGITTARIUS PRACTICES

It's also important to notice when you expect disappointment because of unresolved pain or trauma. When we have gone through a frightening situation in the past, we may lose meaning in life right now and expect negativity. We lose hope, and that can cause us to focus on the negative or even expect that it will occur again without evidence that it actually will.

Where are you expecting disappointment in your life?

_____

_____

_____

_____

_____

_____

_____

How can you heal your heart and hope again?

_____

_____

_____

_____

_____

_____

_____

How can you resist the urge to expect the worst and instead focus on the positive, even if it's small at first?

_____

_____

_____

_____

_____

_____

_____

SAGITTARIUS PRACTICES

Fear is contagious, and we often absorb it from the people around us sharing stories of their lives. When we hear of someone else's trauma—whether it be in the news, social media, or real life—we instantly think it could happen to us. We take on the other person's energy and visualize scenarios in which their trauma happens to us. It's important to recognize what fear is yours and what you are absorbing from the world around you. It's also important to create boundaries around yourself, especially if you know you are vulnerable to certain fears.

What fears have you taken on from the world around you? How can you protect yourself from other people's fearful vibrations?

_____

_____

_____

_____

_____

_____

_____

_____

_____

_____

_____

What can you tell yourself to help you focus on a life in which this fearful scenario does not exist? How can you stay present with your reality?

_____

_____

_____

_____

_____

_____

_____

SAGITTARIUS PRACTICES

_____

_____

_____

_____

_____

_____

_____

_____

Fear can also have no known cause. Sometimes we just fear things, like public speaking. We don't know why we have the fear, but it prevents us from doing something we want to do. Perhaps it's a result of a previous life but has no place in this one. The best way to deal with this type of fear is gentle exposure. Do the thing that scares you without overwhelming yourself. Take baby steps, but resist the urge to avoid what scares you. When we avoid our fears completely, it tells our brains that we can't handle them. Instead, teach yourself that your fears have no power and that the thing you were once scared of really isn't that scary.

How can you gently expose yourself to certain fears without overwhelming your senses?

_____

_____

_____

_____

_____

_____

_____

_____

_____

_____

_____

SAGITTARIUS PRACTICES

Is there something you strongly want to do but feel blocked by fear for no apparent reason? How can you do it despite your fear? What will help you feel safe and strong through this process?

_____

_____

_____

_____

_____

_____

_____

_____

_____

_____

This Full Moon is the perfect time to start on the path of exposing yourself to your fears. Pick something to do today that helps you take control of your life and face your worries. Start with a small step, but commit to taking steps each day. Feel the potential of your life and identify which fears are holding you back from that potential. Break through the confines of your mind and take a leap of faith. Align with the optimism of Sagittarius to trust that the best will always occur.

What would you do if fear wasn't an issue?

_____

_____

_____

_____

_____

_____

_____

SAGITTARIUS PRACTICES

_____

_____

_____

_____

_____

_____

_____

What leap of faith is calling you?

_____

_____

_____

_____

_____

_____

_____

_____

What daily practices can help you do the thing that scares you but will change
your life?

_____

_____

_____

_____

_____

_____

_____

_____

_____

LAST QUARTER
IN PISCES

MAY 30TH

The Last Quarter is the final phase of the lunar cycle. The energy of this Pisces Moon is here to bring closure to any in-progress releases that started on the Full Moon. This is another chance to cleanse ourselves of anything that is taking up space in our psychic bodies so that we can create room for our dreams to materialize. At this time, any inhibiting self-talk, habits, and fears can be cast away. We often harbor these frequencies in our internal systems to cope with pain and trauma, but when they start to feel more like resistance than protection, we are ready to shed these layers. The Last Quarter Moon can be very healing, and with Pisces energy coming around for the second time in one Sun Season, there is double the amount of restorative power to support you through the process.

Pisces is the healer of the zodiac. Much like the ocean that rules it, the sign carries an ability to be both fierce and graceful, expansive and yet embracing. If you align with this theme and trust that you can release your burdens into its vast waters, you will also be held by these waters. You are divinely supported, even when you cannot see a clear path ahead. Pisces creates a gentle, compassionate space where we can sit with our experiences and recognize that whatever we are currently going through is temporary. Just like the changing tide, nothing in life is constant. So instead of ruminating on our emotions, can we practice simply observing and learning from them?

This is a time to trust in the flow of your life. And when you are not in flow, try to name what is weighing you down. While the familiar may be comforting, it may also hinder your ability to experience a greater trust in yourself and the Universe. What if a new level of joy lies on the other side of your comfort zone? When we let go, we open up a multitude of possibilities for something better to enter our lives.

Harness the Piscean energy of this Last Quarter Moon by being present with water. If you live near a body of water, it would be beneficial to spend time in or around it. A bath can also achieve the desired effects. As you find yourself in this water, surrender to its magical qualities and let it cleanse you of any lingering clutter that was not released on the Full Moon. As the energetic debris dissolves into the water, be at peace knowing that you will be intentionally filling this space again during the next New Moon.

When the moment feels right, take out your journal. Visualizing and embodying the properties of water, write "I feel" at the top of the page. Allow the rest to pour out of you in a stream of consciousness and decline the urge to censor or judge your expression. Give yourself the space to process things you may not have fully realized until this moment. When you are finished, do not rush on to another task. Sit in this moment and focus on your breath, moving your energy through your body and feeling your full potential.

AFFIRMATIONS

Take a moment and envision taking a leap of faith. What what-ifs or worst-case scenarios come up? What fears come up for you when imagining the unknown?

Write three to five affirmations that counter these what-ifs. You can write positive what-if statements that assume the best will happen, like "What if everything works out?" Or you can write "I am" statements that remind you of your strength and ability to persevere in any situation.

HAPPY
FULL MOON!

Thank you to everyone who supported and purchased this workbook.

Special Thanks to Rebecca Reitz (rebeccareitz.com, @becca_reitz) for her beautiful artwork on the cover & pages 2, 4, 6, 9, 20, & 32.

For a monthly subscription contact hello@spiritdaughter.com or visit www.spiritdaughter.com.

Disclaimer: The exercises and yoga sequences in this book are physical activities that should be performed carefully to avoid injury. You agree to accept all risks and release Spirit Daughter and any guest instructors from any and all liabilities. Please take care and enjoy.

Follow along our journey on IG:
@spiritdaughter

We always love seeing your photos & hearing about your experiences with the workbooks! Tag us to be featured on our community page:
@spiritdaughtercollective